T0065265

WAIT
'TIL YOU HEAR
WHAT HAPPENED

WAIT

'TIL YOU HEAR
WHAT HAPPENED

ARNETTA BATEMON

WAIT 'TIL YOU HEAR WHAT HAPPENED

iUniverse books may be ordered through booksellers or by contacting:

iUniverse
1663 Liberty Drive
Bloomington, IN 47403
www.iuniverse.com
844-349-9409

Because of the dynamic nature of the Internet, any web addresses or links contained in this book may have changed since publication and may no longer be valid. The views expressed in this work are solely those of the author and do not necessarily reflect the views of the publisher, and the publisher hereby disclaims any responsibility for them.

Any people depicted in stock imagery provided by Getty Images are models, and such images are being used for illustrative purposes only. Certain stock imagery © Getty Images.

ISBN: 978-1-6632-2438-5 (sc)
ISBN: 978-1-6632-2439-2 (e)

Library of Congress Control Number: 2021916448

Print information available on the last page.

iUniverse rev. date: 08/13/2021

*For my friends and family who encouraged
me to find a writer within.*

This story is based on true events.

PROLOGUE

In the 20ᵗʰ century, our country obsessed over designer sneakers and sports apparel. The apparel symbolized success and we became more obsessed with our style than our character. We know this because in 1990, we were willing to pay over $100 for a pair of sneakers. Some sneakers cost as much as $170. In 1986, an average pair of sneakers cost only $20.

As a result, there was an outbreak of crime among kids who were trying to look "fresh" but could not afford the gear.

According to Elijah Anderson, who works at a college studying how different people behave, only kids in the city were having problems about symbolizing their success by wearing sports gear.

And it wasn't just shoes. Kids were mugged for all types of gear, including bomber jackets, caps and anything that had a sports logo.

In some places, like Atlanta, Georgia, muggings to get gear happened all the time. In fact, it happened 50 times over a four-month period. But that type of thing doesn't happen in The Town where I am, The Community where I live or near The School where I work. Or a least that is what I thought.

But that is what exactly what happened to someone I love dearly. I want you to keep this in mind while I tell you about The Boy being mugged. And then, I want you to help me figure out why he didn't tell anybody.

To help me tell you the story, I wrote down a few key ideas that will help you follow along. "Characters" will tell you about all the people I mention in the story. And "Locations" will tell you about the places that I mention.

Characters:

The Boy – A thirteen-year-old high school freshman attending a new school.

The Man – A superstar athlete admired around the world for his skill and integrity.

The Woman – The Boy's foster parent, who is also his natural aunt. The one with whom he lived when it happened.

The Stranger – The one who did it.

The Narrator – I am telling you the story the way I see it. I am also The Aunt. I am The Woman's sister.

The Aunt – The one who should really have custody of The Boy.

The Friend - The Boy's closest pal. They hang out everyday.

His Sister - The Boy's older sibling who stays at my house most of the time. Once she was older, she moved on.

His Other Sister – A much older sibling who has her own family.

Locations:

The School - A school in a well-funded school district in the suburbs.

The Community - A serene suburban community with low crime and middle-class values.

1

THE BOY

I love The Boy as though he were my own son. That is an important statement because I do not have kids of my own. In fact, I tried to adopt him. But I didn't quite speak up in time. So, I get to be a good second Mama whenever I have the opportunity. The Boy is a lovable kid. As a baby, he rarely cried. He had just the right amount of plumpness to make me want to hug him all the time.

As The Boy grew older, he simply grew cuter. The baby boy had a ready smile with a dimple in cheek. When I would talk to him, he would coo and giggle, letting me know he just couldn't wait to have conversations with me. He was well spoken at an early age. Even as early as three years old, he could clearly ask for a "potkissle". I guess the word popsicle is a bit of a tongue-twister for a three-year old.

The Boy is usually mild mannered, following directions the first time and never talking back. I remember one time when I was cooking, he was being a typical little boy by aggravating His Sister. When she yelled out for help to make him stop, all I had to do was let him know that I would drop him in the pot and cook and eat him. He stopped right away, and with pure belief and utter horror, yelled, "I don't want to be eaten!" I could hardly wait for him to leave the room behaving nicely, so I could burst out laughing at his naivety.

He's great company, too. At least I like to think so. I am filled with joy just having him around and hearing his laughter as I move around the house. His contagious laugh brings me running to the room to find out what's going on.

The Boy is filled with love towards the people around him. He adores His Sister, who is one year older than he is. I believe he values his relationship with her more than anyone else. Now isn't that something to be admired? Knowing that he loves her that way makes me love him that much more.

His Sister usually stays at my house, which is why I was just a little slow to volunteer to have stay as well. I wanted to be sure I would be able to care for not one, but two young children, all of a sudden. I had to change around my schedule and change the way I work, but I certainly wanted to help out and do whatever I could.

The Boy is growing older now and it has been an exciting journey to share in his upbringing. When he wasn't with the "The Woman" who took him into foster care, I was usually hung out and played "Mommy".

Let me pause right here to tell you a little bit about "The Woman". She is the mother of two and she has grandchildren, with whom I also have a special relationship. During tough times, we could count on one another. And although we disagreed on some major issues, we always seemed to see eye -to -eye about children needing unconditional love. Since she already had children, I really thought she would step aside and let me have custody of The Boy. But I assume she had her reasons for wanting him for herself.

To this day, I still want to believe I could have done a better job of having him full time. The Woman and I differ in our approach about school and extracurricular activities. I was always a stronger student than The Woman. So, I placed more importance on The Boy doing well in school, since he is such a quick learner. The Woman is slightly more fun than I am. She likes to make sure he sees different parts of the world, so she plans a lot of vacations, which is also important. Sometimes it is good to strike a balance of all the important things in life. Through it all, I am happy to be a part of his life.

Earlier I mentioned how much of a joy it was to hear his laughter around the house. Later on, that became the joy of hearing him sing around the house. The Boy has a nice voice and I smile every time I hear him sing. It would be nice to help him to develop his interest in singing and playing musical instruments. But that might be one of those things that The Woman did not think was a good idea. She once told me he could walk home if he wanted to stay after school for activities. I personally know how difficult it is to lug instruments and bookbags back and forth to school. But unfortunately, I was not available at the time of day to pick him up from school. So, The Boy had to give up playing the drums at school for the moment. He would start back up later.

Having thoroughly explained how much I love The Boy, I want to let you know that doesn't make him perfect. He has done his share of mischief just like any other boy. Just to let you know how normal he is, he was caught throwing rocks by one of my neighbors. She saw him tossing gravel towards her car. And even though the car was already dented where the gravel hit it, I felt obligated to ground him.

A few years later, he began to experiment with the type of friends he would like to have. He happened to choose a couple of friends who thought taking things from the local K-Mart was fun. Well, guess who got caught. The Boy. He was detained by the store police officers who told him he would go to juvie if no one came to pick him up. Fortunately for him, I was home and drove to the store right away to get him. After I gave him a stern lecture in the car, he cried, showing his regret. I wasn't mean about it, but I clearly explained all the risks he was taking by behaving that way. He had to pay a fine and stay away from the store for a while. Let's think about it. He had $5 to pay for the item. So, what would make him do a thing like that? Was it to try to be cool in front of the other boys? Like I told you, he had his share of mischievousness and his shortcomings.

I think I have given you a good idea of my relationship with The Boy. I also think I have painted a good picture of what type of kid he is. We have a loving and considerate relationship, which has his best interest at the center. That's why I thought I had stacked up my cool points after the way I handled the K-mart problem.

But, since he didn't tell me when The Incident happened, I understand we still had a way to go in that regard.

2

THE MAN

Everybody loves The Man. As a superstar athlete, he is admired around the world by men, women and children. He is known for his extraordinary skill. The Boy is not an exception about admiring him. Even though the height of The Man's career did not occur during The Boy's generation, The Boy still developed a keen awareness of The Man's skills and mega fame. The Man's skills are phenomenal, dazzling the crowds and keeping his competitors in awe.

During his college career, he was already being recognized as the next great thing that would happen in the sports world. He was pursued by professional teams throughout the country. When he landed in one of the entertainment capitols of the world, that only added to the admiration The Man already received.

His fans are a group of people who copy him as much as possible through haircuts, gear and well-made attempts at sports. People dedicate hours each day trying to achieve a fraction of the skill The Man demonstrates. The Man has been the role model for several other athletes that went on to achieve their own greatness in sports. Other athletes measure themselves by the records that he has set. I imagine that must be a lot of social pressure, but he seems to handle it like a real pro.

In fact, people from all walks of life hold him up as a role model. The Man is a symbol for how hard work can pay off. Heck, I admire him myself. Outside of sports, he seems to be a role model for excellence, dignity and all the qualities that parents would find respectable. That just ups his points on the cool scale.

The Man has taken his sport to an art form. He has become a brand, like Pepsi or KFC. He'd have to be to make The Shoes become so popular. (I'm gonna tell you about those Shoes a little bit later).

The Boy also caught on to the frenzie and began to sing The Man's praises and participating in the craze. It makes me laugh when I hear him arguing with his friends about The Man's food points. When I look at The Boy, his features even slightly resemble The Man. The fact that he dresses in the team's colors, wears the gear and tries to dress like a sports star would, adds to the resemblance.

Although I have not had many opportunities to watch him do his thing, I must say that when I do, The Man certainly stands out among athletes.

I wonder how The Man would feel if he knew about The Incident.

3

THE SHOES

As I mentioned before, fashion retailers designed clothes for The Man. In particular, shoes were made The Man in mind. When these shoes first hit the scene, it only increased the awe that people already felt about The Man. The Shoes were stylish, yet athletic. The style of The Shoes was already creating a craze, but when they were especially designed for The Man, everybody went wild.

The shoes seem to heighten the excitement about The Man's athletic abilities. The fans would speculate about the abilities of the shoes and whether they contributed to his phenomenal skills. So of course, people would only rush to the store to get a pair of The Shoes. Why? Because we all want to be "phenomenal".

It goes without saying that they were not the cheapest shoes on the market. But for those who bought them, it was like owning a piece of The Man himself. The Shoes were a tremendous source of pride for people who wore them. The Shoes were some of the first athletic shoes to be issued in a variety of styles and colors.

In fact, it was almost a necessity to own at least one pair. That was the way to earn your cool points. And those who could afford more than one or two pairs, earned leader of the crowd status, to be envied by on-lookers.

Although it has become more ordinary to see The Shoes, they are still a source of pride. It is still considered to be just as cool today as it was when the craze first began. People still buy many pairs of The Shoes, creating a shoe wardrobe to match their favorite team's gear or just color-coordinating their outfits. The Woman seems to agree that owning several pairs of The Shoes is a good idea. Yet, The Boy doesn't have any after school activities. Does that seem odd to pay that much for shoes and not make good use of them?

Today, even more athletes have cool shoes on the marking creating more choices to earn cool points based on fresh gear. And even though The Shoes are still considered stylish and trendy, people could easily buy similar shoes about a different athlete. After all, The Shoes have been on the market for a while now, so we ought to be used to them.

Or so I thought. And then The Incident happened. I may be more amazed than The Boy that such a thing would occur.

4

THE WOMAN

One of the most interesting parts of this story is The Woman, who is my sister. She is 11 years older than me. Over the years, I picked up a thing or two from her about how to have fun and keep children happy. One of my first jobs was babysitting her children. I learned a lot about how to be a Mommy around her children. This is one of the benefits of having an older sister.

Let's see, "What are her good points?" She can be reliable. I have had a few emergencies throughout my years, and she has always been there. She likes to have fun and be filled with laughter. When she wants to, she can be loyal and trustworthy. And those characteristics are important in any relationship.

She has seen some trials in her time. She puts on a strong front and pretends she is not bothered. Is it any wonder that she didn't tell me right away?

The Woman is the natural mother to a boy and a girl. These are the children I babysat when I was younger. We have a lot in common when it come to having fun with youngsters. We both enjoy playing with them and singing to them. Together, we take have taken children on trips to amusement parks, water parks and picnics. The Boy's favorite seems to be amusement parks. He looks forward to taking numerous trips each summer. Like I said, The Woman enjoys planning vacations.

So, it's fair to say that she does enjoy being around children. At least, for a short time. She has never been much of a babysitter for other people, so I was a little surprised when she took The Boy home with her full time. But after I saw how she cared for him, I knew that he would feel loved.

Over the years, The Woman has faced a few challenges that made people talk about her the wrong way. I always tried to be supportive towards her. But The Woman is competitive, so I know it bothered her a great deal to know people were "meddling in her business" and talking about her. Having The Boy may have eased some of that for her. He gave her new reasons to feel important.

So, I guess what I am trying to say is that The Woman can be a little crafty sometimes in getting what she wants for whatever reason she may want it. I have never asked her about this. I have only observed what has happened over the years.

One of The Woman's strong suits is arguing. She loves having the last word and she generally does not listen to anybody trying to persuade her to look at things a different way. That's one place where we are different. I tend to overlook most reasons to disagree with her. I may have been wrong to do so about The Boy. I should have insisted on being the one to adopt him. But I figured I would always be a part of his life. After all, I had worked really hard to earn my cool points.

So, what I did instead is share. I made sure The Boy felt welcome to stay for extended sleep overs, even though it did not happen very often. After all, I usually had His Sister and would make a point of taking her to visit him when he was available.

5

THE AUNT

How do I describe myself? There are many words I would like to use, but let's just focus on those that would apply to how I feel about The Boy.

I was loving, generous, fun, and always there for him. I like to believe that I taught him valuable lessons about life that would guide him in making the right decision later. I wanted to help him understand how to think about things, so he could make the best decisions for himself. I showered him with love and genuine attention. After all, he is one of my favorite people.

I was there since the beginning. I wanted to adopt The Boy for myself. But The Woman beat me to the punch on that one. So, I settled for being around as much as I could. I would keep The Boy during vacations, after work, overnight and on weekends whenever I could.

For the first time, I arranged my home to make it more child-friendly. I began to store toys and kids' movies at my house. I enjoyed watching The Lion King and Barney just as much as he and His Sister did. It gave my pure joy to sit down and spend my time enjoying a movie or reading a book with them. They were so receptive to being entertained and made to feel happy. Their laughter was contagious. They were good company, and I did not mind staying in just to be with them.

Now keep in mind, I am single woman with a career and a schedule that I keep. I had learned how to fill up my time with people to see and things to do. My life was pretty routine. I did not live like I had children around. Even though I really believed that one day I would have children around. For that reason, The Boy and His Sister seemed like an advanced blessing. They would be like a big brother and sister to my own children when I had them.

I was honest when they asked questions and I took my time to explain things in a way that young children could understand. I wanted us to have a good relationship. I wanted them to feel as though he could trust me. Especially in the tough times. But when The Incident happened, The Boy did something totally different. He did not say ONE WORD to me about what happened.

I had worked hard to make sure he understood how much I cared about him and wanted him to trust me. Even though, my sister was ill and unable to care for him personally, I wanted that idea to be as invisible as possible. So, I tried to love him enough for the both of us. I thought that would put enough cool points in the bank for us to have an open and honest relationship.

So, let's just say, I am surprised and a little disappointed because he did not tell me about The Incident when it happened.

6

THE SCHOOL

The School is part of the top-ranking school system in the state. Located in an area filled with business professionals and community leaders, The School attracts students from the families of young professionals. Compared to other schools, The School is big, even by today's standards. It looks like it is about half-a-mile long and houses thousands of students. The Incident occurred right outside The School.

The first time I worked at The School, I was unprepared for how awesome the size of the school was. For the first time, I noticed the buses parked in a row that seemed to be at least two blocks long. Even though, I frequently drove by it, I had never considered what it would take to run a place like that. Well, I learned that it would take actual uniformed police officers just to direct traffic. Whatever happened to The School security guard? As large as The School was, it was run like a well-oiled machine, smooth with very few problems.

For most, it creates a good feeling to be a part of something so magnificent. I suppose some students would have difficulty finding their places or feeling comfortable, socially. But not The Boy. He seemed to fit right in. He found his group of friends and began to explore his curiosity. Of course, all his friends wore The Shoes, too.

The district had a budget to be admired and the classrooms were well supplied. It was easy to see the effort to make learning an exciting and cool experience.

The staff at The School is young and hip. And the teachers are aware of the latest trends that grab the interest of the students. Some of them could even be seen wearing The Shoes at work. That's just a sign of how popular The Shoes are. They are considered acceptable apparel for teachers to wear. Doesn't that sound like a cool place to learn?

The Boy once told me that he enjoyed being a student at The School. I think I might know why. It wasn't so much that he enjoyed the classes, as it was a chance to spend time with "her". I saw The Boy with "her" in the hallway between classes. She was cute, with long dark her and big round eyes.

I could tell he really liked her. He was always sure to spend his allowance buying a little piece of jewelry or some other trinket for her when we were out shopping. That's how I know for sure that he didn't have to take anything at K-Mart. He had his own money.

The students in The School, (including The Boy), are receptive to the teachers and generally show a lot of respect for the idea of school. Their behavior makea it easy to assume the responsibility for their well-being. The students are trusting and depend on adults to take responsibility for them. And I didn't mind that they felt that way since several of my younger cousins, nieces and nephews were students, as well. So, the matter was personal for me. As far as the other students, I grew to love them too. I enjoyed working with the students and felt that The School was an important part of The Community.

Don't get me wrong, The School was not utopia. The School still had its share of mischief. I can remember the day that a fight broke out at the end of the school day. It seemed every student in The School rushed through the cafeteria to watch. In that moment, I realized the greatness of the student population. Nothing could be heard over the loud clamor as the students yelled and ran through the hallways. Teachers were not able to penetrate the crowd to break up the fight. By the time I got through the crowd, it was finally breaking up and students were heading for the buses. The whole thing lasted about two minutes.

And even though the fight happened, I still can't believe that any one of the students from The School could be involved in something like The Incident.

7

THE FRIEND

I don't know what to tell you about The Friend. All I know is that I began to trust him around The Boy less and less. In the beginning I thought he would be the perfect playmate. He was about the same age as The Boy, about the same size as The Boy, lived in The Community and attended The School.

The Friend was a smart kid, bringing home A's and B's on his report card and well behaved in school. They had the same interests and could entertain one another for hours. They seemed like the perfect pair.

The Friend was equally adorable as The Boy. He had a ready smile and a need for love and approval. The Friend was in classes for gifted children at school. It put me at ease to know The Boy had a friend that was so similar to him. I figured it would create a positive influence and an ideal situation for both of them to grow into decent young men.

As the years went by, and The Boy grew mischievous, it seemed The Friend was always around. But here is the tricky part, it seemed The Friend never got caught doing anything that he shouldn't, yet he was always there when the trouble broke out. Now keep in mind they are like two peas in a pod. What one does, the other one does. You might wanna call them "Frick and Frack". How likely is it that only one of them would ever get into trouble?

As time went on, I became more suspicious of The Friend and wanted The Boy to spend less time with him. The Boy must have told The Friend, because he began to be a little more distant and less respectful. It was either that or I was dead on in my suspicions that The Friend was intentionally leading The Boy astray. Nevertheless, I treated him with the same regard, because I didn't actually have any proof that he was misleading The Boy.

Even after The Incident happened, it took The Boy a little while to cool off and realize that The Friend was always there, yet The Boy was the only one who caught trouble. When The Boy stopped hanging with The Friend, trouble seemed to disappear.

8

THE COMMUNITY

As I mentioned before, The Community is a place where young professionals and their families live. It is close-knit community where people attend neighborhood churches and shop at the local grocery store. Neighbors take responsibility for one another and show interest in each other lives. Members of the community think alike and place value on the same ideas. These are ideas like family, priorities and religion and school.

The Community is home to many new neighborhoods that have neatly trimmed yards, tree-lined streets and garage sales on Saturday morning. It seemed like an ideal place to live and like everyone was happy. The type of place where one would see little league games and dog-walkers while driving down the street. Normal, wouldn't you say?

I can remember having a family picnic at the public park in The Community. The Boy was a little younger then. Maybe about 7 or 8. We swam and ate while the kids played in the park. It is one the rare occasions when I did not feel like I had to watch The Boy because I was overly concerned about his safety. I relaxed while we were having fun in the park located in The Community.

The Community was the type of place where everyone had the same sense about family and understood each other that way. In a place like the park, everyone would take responsibility for the safety of the kids who were out playing. That is why I could relax and enjoy myself.

My sister, The Woman, is a part of The Community. She seemed very satisfied with her choice of where to live. One of my old friends from high school lived a few doors down. My sister knew her and somehow I think it helped make her feel comfortable about living in The Community.

We would gather at her house for barbecues and volleyball in her large back yard. They were good times. In The Community, big back yards filled with swing sets and swimming pools were normal.

Although, I still felt that I would have been a better choice for The Boy, I was happy with the environment she provided for him. The Community represented enough stable family values that I could relax about his well-being.

No one would think The Community was the type of place where one would expect something like The Incident to happen. The Boy was living with The Woman and attending The School in The Community when The Incident occurred. That's why it was such a surprise when the Incident happened.

9

THE INCIDENT

Well, The Boy decided to stay there in The Community and attend The School. At this point in his life, The Boy was used to wearing a pair of The Shoes to school each day. Freshmen year is usually the first year the students can wear street clothes. So, the students like to be stylish and sport the latest trends. And "everybody" should have a pair of "The Shoes." The Boy could sport a different pair of The Shoes every day of the week.

The Boy usually walked home with The Friend, since The Woman's house was within walking distance of The School. His route home would let people see his sporty apparel as they were passing by on the street.

He was attending school in a new building, with new people and he was a "freshie". So, he was going through a few adjustments. Wearing The Shoes and the latest gear gave him confidence. Looking good was one less worry The Boy had while he was getting used to attending The School.

Having The Friend around was another source of confidence for The Boy. I am sure he felt as though he had someone around whom he could trust and who would understand the pressure of being a "freshie". Walking home with The Friend was one the highlights of his day. They enjoyed each other's company while they compared the events of the day.

The Boys were enjoying their first year in high school and used the walk home to entertain one another talking about events of the day. On a lazy October afternoon, The Boy and The Friend were leaving school and taking their usual route home. As they strolled home, laughing and talking, taking their safe, suburban surroundings for granted, they failed to see The Stranger approaching them. He walked up to The Boys and asked for money. As The Boys tried to shrug it off and keep going, The Stranger became frustrated and angry after repeatedly being told no. So, he drew his arm back and punched The Boy in his face. As The Boy staggered from the strength of the punch, The Stranger repeatedly punched him, causing The Boy to fall to the ground. The Boy tried to defend himself but The Stranger was older and more experienced about fighting. The Stranger punched harder and showed more anger and determination. The Stranger kicked The Boy as he lay on the ground. The Stranger removed The Shoes from The Boy's feet and took the money from The Boy's wallet. The Stranger ran away as The Boy laid on the round bloodied and bruised from the beating. The Boy looked around for The Friend, but he had run away as soon as the fight started.

The Boy crawled to his feet and stumbled to a nearby home to get some help. He called The Woman, who then called an ambulance.

10
WHEN EVERYONE FOUND OUT WHAT HAPPENED

The Boy stayed in the hospital overnight. The doctor bandaged him up pretty good and sent him home. The Woman didn't bring The Boy around for a while and if anybody asked, she would just say he was fine and hanging out with The Friend. The next time The Woman actually brought The Boy around, The Boy had healed, and no one could tell he had been in a fight right away. He was beginning to grow a little mustache, so the scar at the corner of his mouth was hidden. No one would guess The Boy had been beaten. The Boy, The Woman and The Friend kept the secret. Time went by and everything returned to normal.

And then one day, The Woman let it slip that The Boy had been in the hospital. This was over a year after The Incident happened. Of course, I had to know all the details about the secret that had been kept from me.

After hearing what happened, quite naturally I was horrified. Knowing what I did about The Community and The School I was amazed that anything like that would ever happen there.

It was heartbreaking to hear what happened to The Boy. I felt more protective of The Boy. And even though The Boy basked in the attention, at the same time he became more distant and withdrawn. After The Incident, his behavior changed. He didn't seem to focus on school as much and he began to struggle more with his coursework. He seemed to be in more a hurry to grow up and make his own decisions. And most importantly, he made a decision to move away from The Woman. He went to stay with His Other Sister and transferred schools.

It all seemed a little odd. Most people would grow closer to those who love and support them after something like that happened. But that did not seem to happen with The Boy. I am not sure why. But it leads me to believe that he was more disturbed by The Incident than he let on. He also kept hanging around The Friend, even after The Friend had abandoned him during the fight. That let me know The

Boy was a little confused about how to choose what was important.

Now that I have told you all this, wait 'til I tell you what really happened. And then you might understand why all of this went down that way it did.

As it turns out, The Boy, The Stranger and The Friend all knew one another. They regularly hung out in the basement of a home near The School. In the basement, The Boy learned how to keep secrets and tell lies. In The Basement, The Boy learned about things he would have never learned at home. The Boy was losing his youth and his innocence and doing things he knew he shouldn't do. In the Basement, is where he spent time with the friends who were at K-Mart when he was caught stealing. In the Basement, he and The Friend wasted their time instead of engaging in positive activities that would keep them out of trouble.

And I believe that is why The Boy didn't tell anybody that he knew The Stranger who had beaten him. The Boy figured everybody would know that perhaps he wasn't so innocent anymore. Perhaps there would be disapproval about his behavior. And perhaps he thought we would love him less if we knew he had been misbehaving, since we all seemed to dote on him. But that wasn't true.

I eventually sat The Boy down and talked to him. That's when I found out no one had called the police and The Stranger had gotten away with beating The Boy. I thought that was strange that nobody called the police when this happened. I was baffled by the fact that it didn't seem odd to anyone that muggings of little boys were unusual, especially in this neighborhood and perhaps the police ought to look into it.

Furthermore, there was a discount shoe store right across the street. Anybody could get a pair of those shoes real cheap. So why did The Stranger do a thing like that? Why did he shatter the innocence of a young man and set him up to understand bitterness?

I also had to think about my own feelings after this happened. I was hurt. I felt The Boy did not trust me enough to tell me the truth about what happened. Since, it was over a year before I found out anything had happened, I felt left out. I had always thought I was an important part of The Boy's life. And then I thought, maybe the way I showed my love was overwhelming and The Boy did not want to risk not being treated the same way if I knew about The Basement. There could be so many reasons why he would not tell me. I have never asked and he has never told. But I have been around long enough to know that it was not important that he did not tell me. But rather, it was important to know he would be okay. I would just have to put my feelings aside about not being told.

All I know is after The Incident it seemed as though nothing was the same again. He did not talk as much and

I missed his ready smile. The Boy seemed to have lost his vibrancy and the only person he seemed to fully trust was His Sister. It seemed that a great deal of his emotional well-being relied on being around His Sister.

I sometimes thought the change in his behavior was just The Boy changing from a boy to a man, but maybe it was something else. Maybe he was hurt by The Incident more that he showed. All I know is that The Boy has never been the same since it happened.

So, I felt it was more important to love The Boy even more. I found myself wanting to keep him from being hurt again. He eventually came to live with me and of course, attended a different school. He seemed happy and he did not have problems making new friends and fitting in. The Boy even began playing the drums again. That made me believe things were going to be okay. He seemed to get along with being at my house just fine.

And guess what? I still love The Boy just the same, even though he kept this horrible secret. Now, wouldn't you expect your family to do the same with you?

Printed in the United States
by Baker & Taylor Publisher Services